Smoothie Recipes: Over 100+ Smoothie Recipes For Weight Loss

Smoothie Detox Recipes To Burn Fat For Weight Loss

By: Anna Gracey

ISBN-13: 978-1481839037

TABLE OF CONTENTS

Anna Gracey

Publishers Notes

Disclaimer

This publication is intended to provide helpful and informative material. It is not intended to diagnose, treat, cure, or prevent any health problem or condition, nor is intended to replace the advice of a physician. No action should be taken solely on the contents of this book. Always consult your physician or qualified health-care professional on any matters regarding your health and before adopting any suggestions in this book or drawing inferences from it.

The author and publisher specifically disclaim all responsibility for any liability, loss or risk, personal or otherwise, which is incurred as a consequence, directly or indirectly, from the use or application of any contents of this book.

Any and all product names referenced within this book are the trademarks of their respective owners. None of these owners have sponsored, authorized, endorsed, or approved this book.

Always read all information provided by the manufacturers' product labels before using their products. The author and publisher are not responsible for claims made by manufacturers.

Kindle Edition 2012

Manufactured in the United States of America

DEDICATION

I want to dedicate this book to Amy, she has been a complete inspiration to me and has been supportive in writing this book.

CHAPTER 1- INTRODUCING SMOOTHIES

What exactly is a smoothie?

A smoothie (*spelled smoothy in some places*) is a blended beverage that is thick and has a consistency like a shake. Typically a blender is used to puree vegetables and/or fruits in addition to adding liquids like milk, vegetable juice, fruit juice and yogurt.

A Smoothie Has Three Main Components

Typically a lot of smoothies have three main components. There is the liquid (often referred to as the base of the smoothie), ice and a mix of vegetables and/or fruits. If the vegetables and fruits that are used are ice then no ice is required.

Other Ingredients and Thickness

The thick consistency of a smoothie is typically determined by the proportion of solids to liquids. So to make a smoothie less thick more liquid can be added and vice versa. Apart from that a few persons add powders (vitamin supplements or protein powder) to get more flavor and additional supplements. This tends to increase the thickness as well.

Appearance, Garnishes and Toppings

Lemon slices or wedges and fresh mint leaves are some of the types of garnishes used to decorate smoothies. These garnishes are used to make the product more aesthetically appealing especially for the buying consumer.

What Is the Difference between a Shake and a Smoothie?

A few smoothie recipes contain lots of added sugar in the form of chocolate syrup, honey and other additives or even ice cream. Adding all these things would make it a shake instead of a smoothie as a smoothie tends not to have all those added sugars and dairy. They only contain non processed ingredients that are natural.

What is the Difference between a Juice and a Smoothie?

The smoothie is made up of blended or mixed vegetables or whole fruits so a blender is required to make it. On the other hand juices are made by getting the juice out of the vegetable or the fruit. As it pertains to a smoothie the entire vegetable or fruit is utilized along with the added health benefits of the seeds, skin, roughage and other parts that the process of juicing would not include. A smoothie tends to have a much higher nutritional value as it is processed in the same way that juices are.

Smoothie Recipes

Smoothies: Categories and Types

For more than a century individuals have been making smoothies and over that period of time the discovery and inclusion of new ingredients has lead to various categories and types of smoothies being created. They can be roughly categorized as follows:

Green Smoothies- these smoothies are made from dark green vegetables like spinach and tend to be dark green in color.

Fruit Smoothies- fruits alone used to make smoothie especially for the flavor.

Healthy Smoothies- this includes any smoothie that is meant to replace a meal and has all the necessary macro nutrients and vitamins in it.

Dessert Smoothies- these smoothies tend to contain some added fat or sugar in the form of syrups or ice cream. A lot of the recipes that you can find will include added dairy or sugar products to create this dessert and it then is much more similar to a shake.

Weight Loss Smoothies- these kinds of smoothie do not include any added sugars as the aim is to keep the sugar content low. They also tend to be filled with healthy fats like almond butter and flax seed to keep the appetite in check. To augment the process of weight loss stimulants that are coffee based like coffee or green tea can be included as they also curb the appetite and speed up the metabolism.

CHAPTER 2- HOW TO MAKE A SMOOTHIE

When you have been around smoothies long enough and have tried making a few for yourself you will develop your own taste preferences and recipes. In order to learn how to make a smoothie you can simply follow the four basic steps outlined below:

Step 1: Liquid

Begin with one or two cups of liquid. This should be placed in the blender first to ensure that blending process goes well. There are a few types of liquids that can be utilized based on taste and dietary preferences:

The most typical choice is dairy milk. All kinds of milk work as the taste is smooth and flavor neutral.

Soy milk is the best option as it is filled with isoflavones, calcium and protein and contains no cholesterol or lactose and tends to last longer than cow's milk.

Coconut and almond milk are also great alternatives to the others if dairy or soy products are not preferred.

Fruit juices can be utilized to augment the nutrient content of the smoothie. Care has to be taken with the added sugar however as the caloric content will be increased and can inhibit the real fruits natural sugar.

Adding tea means adding antioxidants and caffeine. It is recommended that something is added that does not contain the fruity flavorings or sugar like black tea or green tea.

Caffeine can also be added if coffee is used.

Calcium and probiotics live cultures are added when yogurt is used.

If none of these work for you simply use water.

Smoothie Recipes

Step 2: Vegetables and Fruits

The more vegetables/fruits you use, the less ice you will require. The more juice the vegetables and fruits have the less liquid you will need as well. Bananas are often used in smoothie recipes as they help thicken the smoothie and the taste practically goes with everything. You can try your own combination of fruits and vegetables when you think you are proficient enough. After a while you will realize the ones that really add to the texture and taste of the smoothie.

Step 3: Optional Ingredients

The additional ingredients that you put in the smoothies will help thicken it and make it more flavorful. It is the ideal way to balance the nutrients and give the smoothie that extra kick. A few of the more popular choices are highlighted below:

Protein Powder

This powder will make the smoothie more of a meal. There are quite a number of brands that you can choose from as there are flavors to select. Vanilla is a popular option as it blends well with everything.

Spirulina and Chlorella- these are great sources of vitamins and in terms of weight it is seventy percent protein. The smoothie will also turn green when they are used.

Vitamin Powders- these can be used to supplement the nutritional content of a smoothie. A lot of the stores offer specific powders like those that provide fiber and so on in a powder form.

Vanilla extract, nutmeg. Brown sugar, honey and cinnamon are some of the typical flavorings used to add to the flavor of the smoothie.

A popular addition is ice cream or dairy creamer and when added it makes the smoothie more like a shake.

Almond butter and peanut butter not only provide protein but make the smoothie nice and thick.

Flax and Chia seeds- these are filled with nutrients and omega 3 fatty acids.

Oats provide energy and also help to lower cholesterol.

Step 4: Ice

If you are using more fresh fruit than frozen then you will want to put in a few extra cubes of ice to make the smoothie thicker and cooler. Putting in the ice can also make it less sweet.

Blending

You ought to blend all the ingredients until the liquid is circulating fully in the blender for between five to ten seconds. In other words the ingredients should be liquefied and circulating freely. It can take approximately forty five seconds for all of this to take place based on how full the jar is and how powerful the motor is.

Ensure that you do not fill the jar too much or the ingredients will not liquefy properly even if you have the best motor around. if the blender that you have will not be able to handle fruit that is not cut up or frozen it is recommended that you buy a high end blender for smoothies. It will cut down on the time needed for preparation and blending.

Try It

Smoothie Recipes

If you feel that you are fully prepared to start making your smoothies you are encouraged to follow the tips outlined above and try out some of the recipes included in this book.

Extra Tips

Once you have the basics down on how to prepare a smoothie, you will value the extra tips that are outlined below. These have been put together from years of trial and error and will help make you even more proficient at the task.

Purchase in Bulk

As soon as you decide on which set of ingredients you like the most you can purchase them in bulk and end up saving some money.

Use Ingredients That Are Frozen

Whenever possible use the frozen ingredients as it will end up saving you money by cutting down on the number of trips you make to the store and in the long the frozen does work out cheaper and they can be stored longer as well and are ideal for bulk purchases.

Select lots of "Super Foods"

Try to make use of vegetables and fruits that will really boost your system and provide all the nourishment that you need.

Invest In a High End Blender

Of course a low end blender is cheaper but it will not end up costing you less in the long run. A high end blender though more costly in the initial stages will work out being cheaper in the long run as it is much more durable and better able to handle the chunky fruits and ice that you are blending.

Drink to Remain Healthy

Learning the process of making smoothies ought to be a fun process that is ongoing and is filled with experimentation. It can easily become a part of your daily routine. Don't be afraid to try new flavors and fruits.

CHAPTER 3- WEIGHT LOSS SMOOTHIES

Smoothies are extremely satiating especially if greens are added to them. As a result of this they are the ideal healthy snack for the person on a diet. Opting for a fruit filled smoothie is much better than having some junk food when you begin to feel the pangs of hunger in the early afternoon.

It is a great source of energy prior to a workout. Anytime you make the weight loss smoothie with yogurt, soy milk, milk or ice. Any option will provide you with the necessary amounts of water to keep you hydrated. You will even be able to exercise for a longer period burning more calories in the process.

A lot of nutritionists are of the opinion that fruit smoothies are a great source of healthy fats, oils, vitamins and other kinds of macronutrients that the body requires. Studies indicate that when you take a supplement or vitamin pill the body only absorbs a tiny portion of the nutrients.

When the nutrients are acquired from the vegetables and fruits themselves it will allow a greater portion to be absorbed by the body particularly if they are blended up first which helps the process of digestion.

A juice is not as healthy as a smoothie because a lot of the necessary juices get lost in the process of manufacturing. Juices also do not have as high a fiber content.

If those reasons are not sufficient also note that a smoothie is great for the skin. The copious amounts of antioxidants that fruits like blueberries contain can make the skin glow. The more healthy smoothies you have the greater you will feel and look as well.

Getting a Start

When you just start out with your weight loss smoothies you can stick to the basic recipes at the outset. Simply select on that has no more than two or so ingredients. It will not take long to make and you can be enjoying a shake in less than two minutes. As soon as you become more comfortable making these smoothies you can get into the more complex recipes.

"Super fruits"

It is also best to start out with what are known as super fruits. These super fruits are mangos, blueberries and strawberries. When you have had that for a while you can try out some of the vegetable smoothies (green smoothies).

Smoothie Recipes

These smoothies are made from kale, spinach, lettuce and so on. When combined with fruit the bland flavor of the vegetables will not be tasted and you will get all the nutrients you need without the fuss.

Always remember to keep it simple. The more simple the combination the easier it is to digest. Also use a lot of ingredients that contain water.

As has been mentioned throughout a smoothie will provide you with the necessary nutrients that will enable your body to function more efficiently. Apart from that your energy levels will improve and your skin will be rejuvenated.

With nonfat or low fat yogurt you can get the necessary calcium. You also won't be tempted by the unhealthy sugar filled snacks as that craving will be satisfied.

All in all a smoothie is a perfect way to make the move to a healthier lifestyle. It is extremely easy to get in to the habit and once you have all the ingredients you need you can just put it in the blender and blend. No need to peel anything co no extra preparation time or clean up time required.

Chew Your Smoothies

That was correct. Even though it is liquid chew it (if thick enough) or swish it around in the mouth before you swallow it. Remember that the process of digestion starts in the mouth. The enzymes that are in the saliva help to breakdown the sugars that are found in the fruit.

When you gulp it down it is a big mistake as the stomach will have to work harder to break everything down. A lot of the sugar will get into the bloodstream and increase the levels of glucose which in the long run will make it harder to lose the excess weight.

Don't worry about how weird it feels at the outset, chew the smoothies and you will reap the benefits.

Can Smoothie Be Consumed If I Have Health Issues

This is a question that many choose to ask and to be quite frank the response will be dependent on the health issues that you have. It is best to speak to your health practioners or doctor. They will be able to guide you accordingly. Just ensure that you are consulting someone that can give you the right advice.

The Thicker the Weight Loss Smoothie the Better

I tend to freeze my ingredients beforehand so that I have enough when I need them. When the fruits and veggies are frozen there is no need to add ice and the smoothie will be nice and thick. If you don't want it to be as thick then you can add a few ice cubes. The thicker the smoothie the longer you will stay full.

Smoothie Recipes

Leftovers

You can end up having leftovers when you are done. You can simply place it in the fridge for use later on as it makes a great snack. Another thing you can do is to freeze it by pouring the remaining portion into a Popsicle or ice cube tray and freezing it. They can be had later as a treat.

You can even store the unused portion in the fridge and add it whatever smoothie you are making the following day.

Some Basic Recipes

Banana Smoothie

1 cup orange juice

1 cup yogurt (plain)

1 banana

Cover and blend until smooth.

Blueberry Smoothie

Skim milk (to thin)

8 oz. yogurt (fat free)

1 cup blueberries (frozen)

Place all ingredients in blender then blend. It will have malt like consistency. If the yogurt is plain vanilla and/or Splenda can be added. Lemon or blueberry yogurt can be used as well.

Peach & Banana Smoothie

Anna Gracey

½ cup milk (low-fat)

1 cup peach nectar

1 cup frozen mashed ripe bananas

Place all ingredients in blender then blend to get smooth consistency (thirty seconds). Serve over ice cubes.

Strawberry & Kiwi Smoothie

½ cup strawberries (frozen)

¾ cup pineapple juice

1 cup banana slices (frozen)

3 kiwis (peeled)

Place all ingredients in blender then cover and blend to get smooth consistency.

Fruity Smoothie

1frozen peeled banana (cut in half)

4 or 5 strawberries (frozen) - remove stems

1 six ounce container strawberry/banana or strawberry yogurt

Thaw strawberries and bananas (five to ten minutes) then place all ingredients in blender and cover and blend. Consistency should be smooth.

Berry Banana Smoothie

1 cup yogurt (plain)

Smoothie Recipes

½ cup blueberries

2 bananas

Peel and slice bananas then place them on cookie sheet. Put in freezer then take them out after they are frozen solid and put them in the blender. Put in the blueberries after slicing them and add yogurt then blend to get smooth consistency.

Watermelon Smoothie

3 ice cubes

¼ cup skim milk or soy milk

2 cups watermelon (seedless)

Blend all ingredients then serve.

Berry & Banana Power Smoothie

1 ½ tablespoons soy protein powder or vanilla

Honey to taste

¼ cup sliced strawberries (with stem)

½ small ripe banana (peeled)

½ cup low-fat yogurt (plain)

¼ cup orange juice

Place all ingredients in blender, cover and blend to get smooth consistency.

Mango & Apricot Smoothie

Anna Gracey

6 oz. Mango-Apricot yogurt (light & fat free)

1 cup lemonade (Crystal Light)

½ banana

5 or 6 apricot halves (canned)

Place all ingredients in blender then blend on high for two minutes. Serve in glass.

Banana Apple Soy Smoothie

2 peeled ripe bananas (cut in half)

2 peeled and cored apples (cut in quarters)

10 fl. oz. yogurt (nonfat)

2 tbsp. Splenda or sugar

15 fl. oz. soya milk (organic)

Place ingredients in the blender and blend to get smooth consistency.

Special Smoothie

6-7 ice cubes

1 banana

5-6 blueberries (frozen)

6-7 strawberries (frozen)

4-5 slices peaches (frozen)

½ cup orange juice

Smoothie Recipes

1 tsp. honey (optional)

Dash of nutmeg (optional)

Fresh mint (optional)

Mix all ingredients except the nutmeg, mint and ice cubes in blender then blend to get smooth consistency. Put the ice in and blend again. After pouring in glass sprinkle the nutmeg on and add fresh mint as garnish.

Orange Strawberry Banana

Handful of ice cubes

½ cup orange juice

½ cup milk

1 cup vanilla yogurt

1 handful of strawberries

1 banana

Place all ingredients in the blender then blend to get smooth consistency.

Banana Blueberry Smoothie

½ cup of ice (crushed)

Pinch of cinnamon (if desired)

¾ cup skim milk

¼ cup vanilla yogurt (nonfat)

¾ cup frozen or fresh blueberries

1 medium banana (ripe)

Place all ingredients in the blender then blend to get smooth consistency.

Orange & Banana Smoothie

6 strawberries (frozen)

8 dark cherries (frozen)

1 peeled and segmented orange (remove white pith)

1 peeled and sliced banana

1 nonfat cherry yogurt (8 ounce container)

Place ingredients in blender the cover and blend to get smooth consistency.

Pineapple Blueberry Smoothie

1 tablespoon sugar

1 nonfat vanilla yogurt (8-ounce carton)

1 cup strawberry-orange-pineapple juice or orange-pineapple juice (chilled)

2 cups chilled frozen or fresh blueberries (thaw slightly)

Place all ingredients in blender then blend for one to two minutes to get smooth consistency.

Simple Smoothie

Smoothie Recipes

½ C. Grape Nuts or 1 bale wheat (shredded)

1 or 2 bananas (small)

1 apple

1 cup grapes

1 cup orange juice

2 cup vanilla or plain yogurt

12 walnuts

If preferred you can add 1 peach, 1 orange, honeydew melon/cantaloupe and dried apricots. Place all ingredients in blender and blend to get smooth consistency.

Kiwi Cantaloupe Smoothie

1 ripe banana

¼ cantaloupe (with skin)

1 peeled kiwi fruit (firm)

Chop up cantaloupe and kiwi fruit the put all ingredients in blender and blend to get smooth consistency.

Apricot & Apple Smoothie

1 Tbsp. honey

10 ice cubes

¾ cup vanilla or plain yogurt (nonfat)

1 peeled banana

4 fresh and pitted apricots

1 cup apple juice

1 peeled, cored and chopped apple (Golden Delicious)

Place all ingredients in blender and puree to get smooth consistency.

Breakfast Punch Smoothie

8 oz. water

1 stalk celery

1 cup parsley (fresh)

⅛ cup Cacao powder

1peeled banana

¼ cup goji berries

1peeled kiwi

Place all ingredients except parsley and celery in blender. For ten seconds blend on high then add the parsley and celery and blend for another thirty seconds or until consistency is creamy.

Berry & Apple Smoothie

12 red grapes (seedless)

7 pre frozen strawberries

2 cubed apples

Place apple and grapes in blender then blend until consistency is smooth. Put in frozen fruit and blend.

Smoothie Recipes

Fiberful Berry Smoothie

3 ice cubes

⅛ teaspoon cinnamon (ground)

1 cup vanilla soymilk (low-fat)

1 cup strawberries (stemmed and halved)

1 cup blueberries

1 cup blackberries

Place all ingredients in blender and blend to get smooth consistency. Splenda or honey can be added if the berries are not ripe.

Avocado & Spinach Surprise

1 tbsp. yogurt (low-fat)

1 tsp. vanilla extract

1 tsp. cinnamon

4 leafs of spinach

3 spoonfuls of avocado

½ cup mango (of pre-frozen)

1 cup of coconut milk

½ peeled banana

Blend until consistency is smooth.

Banana Orange Delight

Anna Gracey

1 cup yogurt (low-fat)

½ cup skim milk or soy milk

1 large peeled banana

½ cup pre frozen strawberries

1 cup orange juice

Blend on high speed until consistency is smooth.

Fruit & Oats Smoothie

2 ice cubes

2 tbsp. coconut flakes

2 tbsp. freshly ground flax seeds

2 cups soy milk

½ cup pre frozen kiwi

½ cup pre frozen strawberries

½ cup oats (rolled)

1 pre frozen banana (peeled)

Fruits should be frozen overnight then blended in the morning on high until consistency is smooth.

Creamy Orange

3 ice cubes

¼ tsp. vanilla

Smoothie Recipes

⅓ cup yogurt (low-fat)

3 tbsp. orange juice concentrate (frozen)

1 peeled navel orange, peeled

Place all ingredients in blender and blend to get smooth consistency.

Super Morning Smoothie

A handful of ice cubes

½ cup of strawberries

½ cup of orange juice

1peeled and sliced banana

Place all ingredients in blender and blend to get smooth consistency

Mango Tango Smoothie

1 ½ cups mango slices (frozen)

1 cup pineapple sherbet

½ frozen chunks banana (chunks)

1 cup pineapple juice

1 cup orange juice

Put all liquid ingredients in blender then add the frozen ones. Blend on mix for thirty seconds then change setting to smooth and blend to get smooth consistency. Serve at once.

Peachy Mango Smoothie

Anna Gracey

2 tablespoons lime juice

1 cup peach nectar

1 large peeled and pitted peach (cut into chunks)

1 cup mango chunks (peeled)

Place all ingredients in blender and blend to get smooth consistency

Grapefruit Smoothie

3-4 ice cubes

1 tablespoon honey

½ cup non fat plain nonfat yogurt

½ cup cold water (preferably refrigerated)

1 large ruby red or pink grapefruit

Fresh mint, chopped to use as garnish (optional)

Peel the grapefruit and remove the pith then section the grapefruit and remove seeds.

Place water and sections of grapefruit in a blender the blend until consistency is smooth. Put in the ice, honey and yogurt and blend again to consistency that is desired.

Pour into classes and use mint to garnish.

Egg & Banana Power Drink

1 tsp raw honey

¼ cup frozen or ⅓ cup fresh blueberries

Smoothie Recipes

½ cup Almond milk

2 raw eggs (organic)

1 Banana

Place all ingredients in blender and mix until consistency is smooth.

To make the milk place ½ cup of raw almonds overnight in filtered water then mix almonds and water in blender to ground out almonds (water will be frothy and white). Strain to remove any remaining pieces of almonds.

Tangy Tomato Smoothie

Ingredients

3 basil leaves

Juice of ½ a lemon

1 cup of tomato juice (small)

2 chopped tomatoes (freeze before using)

To prepare this smoothie put chopped tomatoes in blender than add basil leaves, lemon juice and tomato juice. Blend until consistency is smooth then serve.

Apple & Cucumber Smoothie

Ingredients

1 apple (organic)

10 thick slices of cucumber

Put slices of cucumber in blender then peel and cut up apple into four sections then add that to blender. Blend until consistency is smooth (thirty seconds) then serve.

Green Tea & Peach Smoothie Recipe

½ cup ice cubes

1 tea bag Green

½ a banana

1 large sliced and pitted peach

1 tbsp honey

Brew 1 cup of green tea and place in refrigerator to chill or brew ½ cup of the green tea then chill it with ice cubes. Blend the peaches, banana and green tea until consistency is smooth adding honey for sweetness.

Green Tea and Ice Cream Recipe

This recipe not only has the health benefits if green tea but has that great ice cream flavor. Vanilla works really well but other flavors can be used.

½ cup honeydew melon

½ a banana

1 cup chilled brewed green tea

½ cup vanilla ice cream (other flavor can be used)

Begin by blending the honeydew melon and banana with the tea until it is almost smooth then put in ice cream and blend using low setting for approximately twenty seconds..

CHAPTER 4- CLEANSING DETOX, STRESS REDUCING AND IMMUNE BOOSTING SMOOTHIES

Detox or detoxification is a word that is used a lot nowadays as more and more people become aware that they have to find some way to get rid of all the toxins that accumulate in the body.

A diet of detox or simply a juicing diet can help to get rid of most if not all of the toxins from the body. The number of toxins that you get rid of is dependent on the amount of foods consumed that have cleansing properties and the number of toxins that are prevented from getting into the body for a particular period of time.

We are not able to prevent toxins from entering the body but some of it can be prevented from entering. These toxins can enter the body in many ways:

Too much exercise

Too much stress

Drugs and Medication

Poultry products

Too much sunlight

Pollution in the water and food

Air pollution

Vegetable /fruit juices are natural ways to detox as they provide the antioxidants and nutrients that are required to nourish, repair, heal and cleanse the body. The presence of fibers and enzymes in vegetables and fruits makes the process of the elimination of toxins pretty easy.

After sticking to this diet for a while those who do it tend to state that they have increased levels of energy and they are able to think more clearly, have better digestion and have clearer skin.

The Advantages

The detox program is a very simple thing and you will be extremely surprised with the results. When you are able to include that in the weight loss smoothie recipes you will be able to add more nutritional aspects to it and get the boost that can do wonders for the body. The great thing is that any type of smoothie will do but it works best if you use the green smoothies. A green smoothie simply means that you have more raw green and leafy components which typically include fruits, spinach and nuts. When that is done you will get the optimal benefits. These smoothies can be had at the start of the day or after an exercise session.

The Numerous Options

It is not hard to find the correct set of weight loss detox recipes that are suited for you. Nowadays locating these recipes are even simpler as you can simply search online. As more and more persons start to realize how important it is to get healthy and stay healthy, the smoothie has increased in popularity. Not so long ago you would have had to endure drinking smoothies that had a bad smell and tasted horrible. This is no longer the case and the green smoothies are now absolutely delicious.

How to Make A Great Green Detox Smoothie

You are able to make your own smoothie recipes that not only promote weight loss but detox the body as well. You will simply need to:

Select fruits that are high in fiber

Select fruits that are great for detox. These work by breaking down the mucus in the digestive system and any plaque that is present.

Put in some extra fiber. Wheat, flaxseed, germs and granola are excellent options.

As soon as everything is mixed in the blender you can pour it into a glass. Put in a bit of salt at that time as well. The smoothie will be too salty if added during the blending. It is pretty simple and healthy at that!

Smoothie Recipes

Below are some great recipes for smoothies that can help you to detox naturally.

Though the recipes outlined below are basically safe for mothers that are nursing or pregnant they should not be on a strict detox diet. Other sets on individuals that should not be on a detox diet are those who are terminally ill, have cancer, thyroid disease, an autoimmune disease, kidney disease, are diabetic, have an eating disorder or have anemia and any other chronic condition.

It is essential that a doctor be consulted before you start any detox program.

Recipes

Antioxidant Smoothie

1 cup pomegranate juice (unsweetened)

2 cups frozen berries (mixed)

Mix 1 cup water, juice and berries in a blender then blend to get smooth consistency.

Green Smoothie

½ cup fresh flat-leaf parsley leaves (loosely packed)

1 ripe banana

1 coarsely chopped apple (Granny Smith)

1 cup firmly packed collard greens or kale (remove stems and chop coarsely)

Mix 2 ¼ cups water, parsley, banana, apple and kale/collard greens in blender then blend to until consistency is smooth. Add more water if it is too thick.

Herb, Carrot and Mango Smoothie

¼ cup fresh herbs (basil, tarragon, mint)

1 cup orange juice (freshly squeezed)

1 cup fresh carrot juice

2 cups mango chunks (frozen)

Mix all the ingredients in blender until consistency is smooth.

Coconut Water & Mango Smoothie

Pinch of cayenne powder

2 cups coconut water (unsweetened)

2 to 3 tablespoons fresh lime juice

Smoothie Recipes

2 cups mango chunks (ripe)

Place all ingredients in blender and blend until consistency is smooth

Carrot & Beet Smoothie

2 teaspoons fresh ginger (minced)

2 tablespoons fresh lemon juice

1coarsley chopped ripe pear (red D'Anjou or red Bartlett)

1 coarsely chopped sweet apple (Pink Lady or Honeycrisp)

1 peeled and coarsely chopped carrot (medium-size)

1 peeled and coarsely chopped red beet (small)

Steam carrot and beets for ten minutes or until tender then let cool to room temperature.

In blender place 2 cup water, ginger, juice, pear, apple, carrot and beets and blend until consistency is smooth.

Berry & Orange Smoothie

1 cup raspberries (frozen)

1 cup blueberries (frozen)

2 peeled navel oranges (remove pith and cut into chunks)

Place all ingredients in blender and blend until consistency is smooth

Honeydew Mint & Cucumber Smoothie

¼ cup mint leaves (fresh)

2 tablespoons fresh lime juice

1 cup pear juice

½ peeled and chopped honeydew melon

½ peeled and chopped English cucumber

Place all ingredients in blender and blend until consistency is smooth.

The smoothies that have strawberries and blueberries (natural antioxidants) are great to slow down the signs of aging and reduce stress.

Melon & Lemon Smoothie

1 tablespoon fresh mint (chopped)

1 cup green grapes (frozen)

½ cup lemon yogurt (nonfat)

1 ½ cups honeydew melon (diced)

Fresh lemon juice to taste (optional)

Mix lemon yogurt and honey dew melon in blender then add the mint and grapes and blend until consistency is smooth. Add more lemon juice if desired.

Strawberry Smoothie

Strawberries have a high nutritional value and are a great source of vitamins.

Ingredients

Smoothie Recipes

2 cups ice

1 cup strawberry yogurt or low fat plain yogurt (if nectar is not available)

1 peach (pitted)

½ cup Strawberry Nectar (Jumex)

2 ½ cups strawberries

Place all ingredients in blender and blend until consistency is smooth.

Oat & Blueberry Smoothies

½ -1 cup water

⅔ Cup oats (rolled)

3 -5 dates (dried can be used)

2 frozen large bananas

3 extra ripe kiwi fruits (small)

1 ⅓ cups frozen blueberries

Use extremely warm water to cover dates then leave for about five minutes to let them soften.

Break up bananas in chinks and place in blender with blueberries and kiwi.

Add dates and the water they were soaking in then blend until it is almost smooth.

Put in oats and blend to desired consistency. Add more water if necessary.

What about the Immune System?

You can visualize the immune system as an army with large number of tiny soldiers that work throughout the body. The way that the army if fed will determine how well they can fight the bacteria and viruses that get in.

Having a smoothie on a regular basis can afford you the opportunity to get the extra boosters that you would not normally get from foods that you eat. Smoothies make great snack option sand work well when you are not well enough to eat solid food or simply have no appetite for it.

It is also advised to reduce the amount of alcohol and sugar that is consumed. When too much of these substances are consumed it will inhibit the production of white blood cells and lower the body's ability to fight bacteria and viruses in the body. These negative effects start immediately and can last as long as five hours.

Consume copious amounts of onions and garlic as they are filled with sulfur compounds that stimulate the immune system. Increase the amount of omega 3 fatty acids, zinc, copper, selenium, bioflavonoid, carotenoids, vitamin E and vitamin C that you consume.

Below are some great smoothies that help to boost the immune system. The taste great and provide the protection that you need.

Recipes

Burst of Citrus

Vitamin C can be found in copious amounts in the citrus family. One only needs approximately five hundred milligrams to stave off a respiratory infection. If you are already sick this smoothie can cut the recovery time in half and it helps relieve that sore throat as well.

2 teaspoon raw honey

½ cup vanilla yogurt (nonfat)

1 or 2 inches young ginger (fresh and peeled)

2 limes or ½ lemon (peeled and seeded)

½ peeled and seeded pink grapefruit

½ cup orange juice

Place all ingredients in blender and blend until consistency is smooth.

Pick Me up Smoothie

Blueberries are packed with antibiotic and antiviral compounds that you need when you are not so well. When mixed with mango that contains beta carotene you get adequate protection from free radicals.

1 teaspoon spirulina/chlorella powder

½ cup milk of choice

½ cup mango slices

½ almost ripe banana

1 cup of frozen/fresh blueberries

1 tablespoon of any type of ground nuts (optional)

Place all ingredients in blender and blend until consistency is smooth.

Orange Power

Packed with bioflavonoid and beta carotene it is great for the immune system. There is also the enzyme papain which is a great anti inflammatory agent. Work well for upset tummies.

1 tbsp chlorella/spirulina powder or brewer's yeast

½ cup peeled and seeded oranges

1 cup seeded and sliced ripe papaya

½ cup carrot juice (fresh)

Place all ingredients in blender and blend until consistency is smooth.

Pumpkin & Strawberry Shake

This is a great smoothie that is extremely filling. To spice it up some ginger can be added.

1 teaspoon of spirulina/chlorella (optional)

1 or 2 inches fresh young ginger (scrape skin off)

½ cup pumpkin (steamed)

½ cup fresh/frozen strawberries

½ cup orange juice

Cut pumpkin into cubes and steam for approximately fifteen minutes then let cool. Place all ingredients in blender and blend until consistency is smooth.

The Melon Surprise

This smoothie recipe is extremely refreshing and boosts the immune system. To get the smoothie nice and creamy use frozen yogurt.

Smoothie Recipes

½ cup seeded and cubed honey melon

1 cup seeded and cubed frozen/fresh watermelon

½ cup non-fat yogurt (frozen) any flavor

500 mg vitamin C powder with bioflavonoid

Place all ingredients in blender and blend until consistency is smooth.

ABOUT THE AUTHOR

Anna Gracey has had issues with her weight since she was a teenager and has literally tried every diet on the planet in a bid to find a solution to her problem. After many failures she started to look at smoothies as a solution. They were tasty and could provide all the nutrients and calories that you needed in one cup. There would be no burgers or fried chicken or anything else like that that would pack on the pounds.

She then modified her diet to a healthier one and started to include healthy smoothies in the mix. Some were not as tasty but with some adjustments in the ingredients she got it just right. When she began to see the results of her efforts she decided to share some of the recipes with others so that they too could reap the benefits of her solution.

She is aware that many will have a problem just having a smoothie for breakfast or lunch or even a snack but if it is all done step by step the excess weight will begin to disappear in no time. Pair it with some moderate exercise and the results will begin to show even more quickly.

5775823R00028

Printed in Great Britain
by Amazon.co.uk, Ltd.,
Marston Gate.